Novels for Students, Volume 19

Project Editor: Jennifer Smith

Editorial: Anne Marie Hacht, Ira Mark Milne, Maikue Vang

Rights Acquisition and Management: Margaret Abendroth, Edna Hedblad, Ann Taylor

Manufacturing: Rhonda Williams

Imaging: Leitha Etheridge-Sims, Lezlie Light, Mike Logusz, Daniel W. Newell

Product Design: Pamela A. E. Galbreath

© 2004 by Gale. Gale is an imprint of The Gale Group, Inc., a division of Thomson Learning Inc.

Gale and Design® and Thomson Learning™ are trademarks used herein under license.

For more information, contact

Gale
27500 Drake Rd.

Farmington Hills, MI 48331-3535
Or you can visit our Internet site at
http://www.gale.com

ALL RIGHTS RESERVED. No part of this work covered by the copyright hereon may be reproduced or used in any form or by any means—graphic, electronic, or mechanical, including photocopying, recording, taping, Web distribution, or information storage retrieval systems—without the written permission of the publisher.

For permission to use material from this product, submit your request via Web at http://www.gale-edit.com/permissions, or you may download our Permissions Request form and submit your request by fax or mail to:

Permissions Department
Gale, Inc.
27500 Drake Rd.
Farmington Hills, MI 48331-3535
Permissions Hotline:
248-699-8006 or 800-877-4253, ext. 8006
Fax: 248-699-8074 or 800-762-4058

Since this page cannot legibly accommodate all copyright notices, the acknowledgments constitute an extension of the copyright notice.

While every effort has been made to ensure the reliability of the information presented in this publication, The Gale Group, Inc. does not guarantee the accuracy of the data contained herein. The Gale Group, Inc. accepts no payment for listing; and inclusion in the publication of any organization, agency, institution, publication, service, or individual does not imply endorsement of the editors or publisher. Errors brought to the attention of the publisher and verified to the satisfaction of the publisher will be corrected in future editions.

ISBN 0-7876-6942-3
ISSN 1094-3552

Printed in the United States of America
10 9 8 7 6 5 4 3 2 1

The Portrait of a Lady

Henry James
1881

Introduction

Henry James was an established author when *The Portrait of a Lady* was published. The novel was first published serially in 1880 and 1881, appearing in *Macmillan's Magazine* in England and in *Atlantic* in the United States. The first book edition was published in 1881.

The Portrait of a Lady was widely, and mostly favorably, reviewed. Some reviewers recognized it immediately as James's most important novel thus far, and a few called it a masterpiece. Both of these opinions have been affirmed as time has passed. Many scholars consider *The Portrait of a Lady* one of the greatest novels in modern literature. Its heroine, Isabel Archer, is widely considered one of James's most powerful characters.

The Portrait of a Lady is, above all, Isabel's story. Following the technique of Russian author Ivan Turgenev, James makes Isabel the axis around which the story revolves. All the story's events, and all the other characters, exist only to serve the purpose of revealing Isabel to the reader.

Author Biography

Henry James was born in New York City on April 15, 1843. His father, also named Henry, was a minister who had inherited wealth. His mother, Mary Robertson Walsh James, was devoted to her husband and five children. Henry was their second son. The first, William, became a Harvard professor and a philosopher whose best-known books, especially *Varieties of Religious Experience* (1902), are still read today. The younger children were Garth, Robertson, and Alice.

James's father took the family on an extended trip to Europe the year Henry was born. Henry's childhood was spent traveling between a family home in Cambridge, Massachusetts, and Europe, where the James's spent time in England, France, and Switzerland. In Cambridge and nearby Boston, young Henry came to know the American intellectual and literary stars of the time, including Ralph Waldo Emerson, Henry David Thoreau, and William Dean Howells. He was educated by private tutors at home and abroad until he enrolled at Harvard, where he studied only briefly. Howells, an influential magazine editor, helped James launch his literary career as a critic and writer for magazines including the *Nation* and the *Atlantic*.

In 1876, at the age of thirty-three, James moved permanently to England; he eventually became a British citizen. The meeting of American and European cultures is the predominant theme in his work. James is considered a master of the novel form and one of the leading practitioners of realism, the literary movement that arose at the end of the Civil War as a reaction against romanticism. James's work falls into the category known as psychological realism, in which the significant action in a work takes place inside the minds of the characters.

Although best known as a novelist, James was also a prolific and respected writer of short stories, plays (some were adaptations of his novels), criticism, and travel essays. As was common at the time, many of his novels were serialized in magazines before they were published as books. *The Portrait of a Lady*, first published in 1881, is widely considered the best of his early novels. Other lasting novels of this period include *The Europeans* (1878) and *The Bostonians* (1886). Well-known and still-popular later works include *The Wings of the Dove* (1902) and *The Ambassadors* (1903); James himself considered the latter his masterpiece. Two novellas, *Daisy Miller* (1878) and *The Turn of the Screw* (1898), appear in countless anthologies and remain popular.

Never successful as a student, James finally received honorary degrees from two of the most prestigious universities in the world: from Harvard, in 1911, and from Oxford, in 1912. He died in London on February 28, 1916, after a series of strokes. His ashes are buried in Cambridge, Massachusetts.

Plot Summary

Chapters 1–9

The novel opens at Gardencourt, the English country home of the Touchetts. Mr. Touchett, his son Ralph, and their friend Lord Warburton are having tea. Mrs. Touchett arrives from America with her niece, Isabel Archer. Isabel is a young American woman of marriageable age. Her father has just died, her mother died some time previously, and her two older sisters are already married. Since Isabel is now alone, and since her aunt thinks well of her, Mrs. Touchett has brought Isabel to Europe so that she can become more sophisticated and therefore improve her prospects for a good marriage.

Just before Isabel appears, Lord Warburton tells Mr. Touchett and Ralph that he is bored with his life and will not get married unless he meets an especially interesting woman. When Warburton meets Isabel, he finds her interesting indeed, and he soon falls in love with her. He invites her to visit his home, and Isabel learns from her uncle that Warburton is very wealthy and highly placed socially. Isabel does visit Warburton's home, where she gets to know and like his two admiring sisters. She also finds that Warburton is kind and sensitive.

Chapters 10–14

Not long after her arrival at Gardencourt, Isabel receives a letter from Henrietta Stackpole, an American friend of hers who is in Europe working as a journalist. When Isabel mentions this to Ralph, he invites Henrietta to come stay at Gardencourt, which she does.

As soon as Henrietta settles in, Isabel receives another letter from another American friend, Caspar Goodwood. Caspar wants to marry Isabel and has followed her to England to press his case with her. Isabel, however, is irritated at Caspar for following her and refuses to answer his letter.

The same day that brings Caspar's letter also brings a visit from Warburton, who proposes to Isabel. She likes him but is not ready to settle down. An independent spirit, she wants to see the world and experience more adventure before she closes off her options in life. Although Warburton is both wealthy and kind, the idea of marrying him makes Isabel think only of her "diminished liberty." She gently but firmly rejects him via letter. Her aunt and uncle are baffled by this, as is Warburton, who comes to see her to ask for further explanation of her refusal. Isabel remains kind but firm toward him.

Chapters 15–21

Isabel, Henrietta, and Ralph travel to London together, since Isabel has not yet visited the capital. Ralph has become very fond of Isabel; her vigor and high spirits make her attractive to everyone she meets. Henrietta meets an old acquaintance of Ralph, Mr. Bantling, who quickly becomes her tour guide and companion. Caspar presents himself at Isabel's hotel and presses her to marry him. Isabel tells him, as she told Warburton, that she wants her freedom for the time being. She adds that, if Caspar still wants to marry her after two years, she will consider his proposal at that time.

Ralph receives a telegram telling him that his father is seriously ill. Ralph and Isabel return to Gardencourt, while Henrietta remains in London with Mr. Bantling. A friend of Mrs. Touchett, Madame Merle, is staying at Gardencourt and befriends Isabel. During this time, Ralph and Mrs. Touchett are preoccupied with Mr. Touchett, who is dying. Ralph persuades his father to leave half his estate to Isabel, so that she will be as independent financially as she is in spirit. Ralph is willing to have most of his inheritance go to Isabel because he, too, is ill, and he knows that he will only live a few more years. Mr. Touchett worries, rather prophetically, that having a large fortune could actually endanger Isabel, making her attractive to unsavory men who want her money. Ralph convinces his father that Isabel is too strong and independent to end up a victim.

Media Adaptations

- A film version of *The Portrait of a Lady* was directed by Jane Campion and released in 1996. It stars Nicole Kidman as Isabel, John Malkovich as Gilbert, and Martin Donovan as Ralph. It is available on videocassette and DVD.

- A made for television movie adaptation was directed by James Cellan Jones and broadcast in 1968. Starring Suzanne Neve as Isabel, James Maxwell as Gilbert, and Richard Chamberlain as Ralph, this movie is available on videocassette and DVD.

- An abridged audiocassette recording of *The Portrait of a Lady*, with Gayle Hunnicutt as reader, was published by HighBridge in 1995. An unabridged version with Laural Merlington as reader was published by Brilliance Audio in 1998.

- An unabridged version of *The Portrait of a Lady*, with Laural Merlington as reader, was published by Brilliance Audio in 1998.

Mr. Touchett dies, and Isabel receives her inheritance. Mrs. Touchett takes Isabel to Paris, while Ralph goes south to the Mediterranean, where the climate will be better for his health. In Paris, Isabel spends time with Henrietta and Mr. Bantling, whose travels have brought them to France.

When Mrs. Touchett and Isabel leave Paris, they visit Ralph on the Mediterranean shore. Isabel questions Ralph about his role in her inheritance and expresses concerns similar to those of her uncle that the money might not be altogether good for her. Ralph reassures her.

Chapters 22–35

Mrs. Touchett and Isabel go on to Florence, where Mrs. Touchett has a home. Here they again meet Madame Merle. Madame Merle arranges for Isabel to meet her friend Gilbert Osmond, an American-born man who has lived virtually his whole life in Europe. Madame Merle speaks highly of Gilbert to Isabel, and she has already told Gilbert about Isabel, as well—including the fact that Isabel is wealthy. Indeed, Madame Merle has told Gilbert that she wants him to marry Isabel.

At their first meeting, Gilbert invites Isabel to his home to see his art collection. There Isabel meets Gilbert's fifteen-year-old daughter, Pansy, and his sister, Countess Gemini. Through a conversation between the Countess and Madame Merle, readers learn that Madame Merle is orchestrating the marriage of Isabel and Gilbert so that Pansy will have money and will therefore be able to marry well. (Gilbert has little money but expensive tastes.) The Countess makes clear her objection to the trap that is being set for Isabel, but she does nothing about it.

Ralph has already let Isabel know that he does not like or trust Madame Merle and that Gilbert has no money. Now Mrs. Touchett begins to suspect Gilbert's motives in pursuing Isabel. She does not, though, suspect that her friend Madame Merle is working behind the scenes to bring the two together.

Isabel falls in love with Gilbert for the same reason she is impressed with Madame Merle: both have a very refined manner and are accomplished in all the social graces. They are the epitome of the sophistication that Isabel has been brought to Europe to acquire. Henrietta and Ralph make appearances in Florence to warn Isabel that Gilbert is a dilettante who is only interested in Isabel because she is wealthy and because she will impress his social circle. Isabel remains as independent-minded as ever, insisting that she loves Gilbert. She spends a year traveling, some of it with Madame Merle, and then returns to Italy. Caspar comes to see her, two years having passed, but Isabel rejects him again. Instead, she agrees to marry Gilbert. Mrs. Touchett tells Isabel that Madame Merle has orchestrated the marriage for reasons of her own, but Isabel does not believe her aunt. Ralph also expresses his disappointment and misgivings—specifically that Gilbert will crush Isabel's independent spirit—but Isabel is determined to follow her heart.

Chapters 36–55

Four years have passed. Gilbert and Isabel are living in Rome. Isabel has realized that her friends and relatives were correct in their objections to Gilbert. He is selfish and controlling; he cares nothing for Isabel's ideas or her happiness but instead seeks to mold her into his idea of the perfect wife.

Isabel hears from Mrs. Touchett that Ralph is dying at Gardencourt and wants to see her. Gilbert tells Isabel that her place is with him, not with Ralph. Upset by this, Isabel talks with Countess Gemini. Gilbert's sister takes the occasion to tell Isabel about Gilbert's past: Pansy is not the daughter of Gilbert and his deceased first wife, as Gilbert has always told Isabel (and everyone else). In fact, Pansy is the daughter of Gilbert and Madame Merle. The two had a long affair, and Madame Merle has engineered Isabel's marriage for the benefit of her daughter, Pansy.

Isabel goes to England to see Ralph and admits to him that he was right about Gilbert's marrying her for money and crushing her independence. Ralph now believes that, indeed, the inheritance that he insisted his father give to Isabel has ruined her. Isabel is not bitter but instead seeks to understand what is the right solution for her predicament.

Ralph dies, and Isabel remains at Gardencourt for a time. Both of her former suitors, Lord Warburton and Caspar Goodwood, make final appearances and urge her to leave Gilbert. Isabel returns to her husband, though, because she believes that this is the right thing to do. She feels that if she does not keep her marriage vows, she would be the same kind of person as Madame Merle, whom she now realizes is profoundly corrupt. Isabel now understands that people like Madame Merle and Gilbert only have the appearance of refinement but are actually immoral. Isabel is not willing to be like them.

Characters

Isabel Archer

The novel's central character, Isabel is a young American woman who embodies all the best of what James depicts as American qualities, especially vitality, sincerity, and independence. As the novel opens, Isabel is arriving at the English home of her aunt and uncle. Her father has recently died. (Her mother died previously.) Her aunt, who traveled to the United States after Isabel's father's death, feels that Isabel has more potential than her circumstances in America will allow her to fulfill, and so she brings Isabel back to England with her.

Isabel wins the admiration of everyone she meets, including her cousin Ralph. Ralph talks his dying father into leaving half his estate to Isabel so that she can be free to do as she pleases. In addition to this benefactor, Isabel also has suitors. Caspar Goodwood travels from America to urge Isabel to marry him. Lord Warburton, a wealthy friend of the Touchett family, also wants to marry Isabel. But Isabel's independent nature leads her to reject both men. She finds Caspar boring and turns down Warburton partly because she is not ready to marry and partly because she fears life with him would be too easy. She longs for some adventure—even for some difficulty that will test her resourcefulness and mettle.

Isabel's independent spirit is the driving force in her personality, and it is what propels her into an unhappy marriage. When she falls in love with Gilbert Osmond, her friends and relatives almost unanimously warn her against him. But she refuses to take anyone's counsel but her own and learns too late that she completely misjudged her husband. Her failure to accurately judge Gilbert's character springs from an innocence that is characteristic of youth and also, in James's view, of Americans. Isabel's direct, trusting nature is contrasted to thatof the book's European characters, who have secret pasts and ulterior motives for everything they do.

Although she makes a bad marriage, Isabel is not a tragic character. Once she realizes that she made a mistake in marrying Gilbert, she resolves to bring her strength of character to bear upon the circumstances that she has created by her own free choice. By refusing to leave her marriage, Isabel refuses to adopt the corrupt ways of her European circle. Instead, Isabel intends to graciously and courageously accept the consequences of her unwise decision and to make the best life she can.

Mr. Bantling

An old acquaintance of Ralph, Mr. Bantling meets Henrietta when she is in London with Ralph and Isabel. He becomes Henrietta's companion and guide as she travels around Europe as a journalist.

Countess Gemini

Countess Gemini is Gilbert Osmond's sister. She is well aware of Gilbert's true character and thus has no affection for him, but the two have a familial relationship in spite of this. The Countess catches on quickly to Madame Merle's scheme to get Isabel to marry Gilbert and voices her objection to it, but she doesn't actually do anything to prevent it. Four years after the marriage, at a time when Isabel is distraught over Gilbert's controlling nature, the Countess, out of sympathy, finally tells Isabel the truth about Gilbert's past.

Caspar Goodwood

Caspar is Isabel's American suitor. Having fallen in love with Isabel in the United States, he follows her to England to try to get her to agree to marry him. Isabel sees his persistence as aggression and is only irritated by it. However, the novel's one moment of passion takes place between Caspar and Isabel, when Caspar goes to see Isabel at Gardencourt one last time after Ralph's death. The couple's passionate kiss can be seen as Isabel's belated appreciation of the honesty and simplicity of character that Caspar personifies.

Madame Merle

Madame Merle is a friend of Mrs. Touchett. Isabel first meets her when both women are guests at Mrs. Touchett's home in England just before Mr. Touchett's death. Madame Merle is older than Isabel and very accomplished socially. She is charming and congenial and, as becomes clear only later, adept at manipulating people and events to serve her interests. Isabel is dazzled by Madame Merle's apparent refinement.

Gilbert Osmond

Gilbert Osmond was born in the United States but has lived virtually his entire life in Europe. He has the same qualities as Madame Merle, and Isabel is attracted to both of them for the same reason. Gilbert is an art collector, and he has an air of charm, sophistication, and refinement that greatly impresses Isabel. While all of her friends and relatives see Gilbert for the self-centered dilettante he is, Isabel is completely taken in and falls in love with him.

More than any other character, Gilbert is not what he appears to be. Although he has expensive tastes, he does not have money. Although he is charming and seductive, he does not really care about Isabel. And although he pretends that his daughter is the child of his deceased first wife, she is actually the product of an affair with Madame Merle.

Pansy Osmond

Pansy is Gilbert's daughter, and she is fifteen years old when Isabel meets Gilbert. Gilbert has always said that Pansy is the child of his first wife, who died giving birth to her, and Pansy was brought up in a convent. The nuns have reared her to be a completely obedient child, which pleases Gilbert.

Readers, along with Isabel, learn the truth about Pansy years after Isabel's marriage to Gilbert. Pansy is actually the product of a long affair between Madame Merle and Gilbert, whose first wife did die, but not in childbirth. Pansy does not know that Madame Merle is her mother but has an obvious dislike for the woman. Pansy likes Isabel and is very happy when she learns that Isabel is going to marry her father. Isabel's love for Pansy may be one reason why she returns to Gilbert at the end of the novel.

Henrietta Stackpole

Henrietta is an American journalist and a friend of Isabel. She is the quintessential "ugly American": loud, brassy, and boorish. Although Isabel sees Henrietta's faults, she is loyal to her friend, as Henrietta is to her. And, although Henrietta does not have Isabel's refinement, she is a better judge of people, and she warns Isabel not to marry Gilbert.

Mr. Touchett

Mr. Touchett is Isabel's wealthy uncle. Like most of the novel's characters, he was born in the United States, but at the time of the story, he has lived for many years in England. He comes to care deeply for Isabel and, when he hesitates to leave her half his fortune, it is only because he is afraid that the money will bring her harm rather than good. Mr. Touchett dies early in the novel after letting Ralph persuade him to leave Isabel a fortune.

Mrs. Touchett

Isabel's aunt, Mrs. Touchett, goes to New York after the death of her brother, from whom she was estranged, and decides to bring Isabel back to Europe with her. Mrs. Touchett is a well-meaning woman who shares some of Isabel's independence and, more surprisingly considering her age and her long time in Europe, her naiveté. Her independence is clear from the fact that she long ago set up her own home in Florence while her husband remained in England, since the two did not enjoy the same kind of life. The two crafted an amicable marriage out of visits to each other's homes. Mrs. Touchett's naiveté is clear in her unwarranted trust of Madame Merle. Like Isabel, Mrs. Touchett is impressed with Madame Merle's mastery of the social graces and fails to see that she is corrupt until it is too late to save Isabel from her scheme. Mrs. Touchett does realize the truth before Isabel does, however.

Ralph Touchett

Ralph is Isabel's cousin. He becomes her admirer, friend, and confidant. Like Isabel, he is intelligent and good-hearted. Unlike her, though, he is physically frail. He is also much less naive than his cousin. He understands and condemns the conniving of Madame Merle and others like her.

Because Ralph cares for Isabel and sees her potential to blossom into a sophisticated woman, he wants to do what he can to give her an advantage in life. Ralph is ill and knows that he will not live long, and therefore he persuades his dying father to leave half his estate to Isabel.

Throughout the novel, until his death at the end of the story, Ralph remains Isabel's supporter, although Isabel's insistence on marrying Gilbert causes tension and even a brief rupture in their relationship. It is significant that when Ralph is near death and asks Isabel to travel to England to see him, she does so even over her husband's objections. Isabel also admits to Ralph that she made a terrible mistake when she married Gilbert. These two actions show the closeness and loyalty that Isabel feels toward Ralph.

For his part, Ralph dies feeling that, while he hoped to benefit Isabel by securing a fortune for her, he actually brought about her ruin.

Lord Warburton

Lord Warburton is a friend of the Touchetts who falls in love with Isabel almost as soon as he meets her. He proposes to Isabel, and when she rejects him, he asks for an explanation but then accepts her decision graciously. Since Warburton is not only extremely wealthy but also considerate and kind, Isabel's rejection of him stuns everyone. Isabel's choice of Gilbert over Warburton is a clear sign of her lack of judgment.

Like Caspar Goodwood, Warburton comes to see Isabel at Gardencourt at the end of the novel and, like Goodwood, he is rejected one final time.

Themes

American versus European Character

The contrast between the American character and the European character is a theme that appears throughout James's work. This is not surprising, since it is a contrast he observed throughout his life as an American who spent most of his adulthood in Europe. According to James, Americans tend to be naive, energetic, practical, sincere, direct, and spontaneous, and they value the individual above society. Conversely, Europeans are sophisticated, lethargic, formal, insincere, obtuse, and scheming, and they value society above the individual.

This theme is especially interesting in *The Portrait of a Lady* because most of its characters are Americans who have been living in Europe for varying periods of time. In general, the longer an American-born character has been in Europe, the more European traits he or she has. Gilbert has lived nearly his whole life on the Continent and is completely European in character. James uses him to personify the worst manifestations of European traits. At the other end of the spectrum is Isabel, who is just arriving in Europe as the novel opens. The things that make her distinctively American, such as her energy and independent attitude, are fresh and interesting to the European characters.

They are also, however, the things that lead to her downfall. By refusing to take the counsel of those who care about her, Isabel falls prey to the more sophisticated Europeans who manipulate her for their own purposes.

James does make a moral judgment about which culture produces better people; he clearly portrays the Americans as having more integrity. But he also shows that, taken as individuals, most Americans and Europeans alike have both good and bad qualities. While Isabel is almost wholly admirable and Gilbert is almost wholly despicable, the other characters are drawn in shades of gray. Henrietta is an example of an American whom James portrays less positively. Her American qualities are exaggerated so that her directness is actually rudeness. Her lack of regard for society and convention is so extreme that she offends as routinely as Isabel enchants. Lord Warburton, on the other hand, exemplifies European qualities in their most positive form. He is sophisticated and conventional, but he is also courteous, sensitive, and gracious even in defeat. Ralph is also a positive European character, a physically weak man who is nevertheless morally strong.

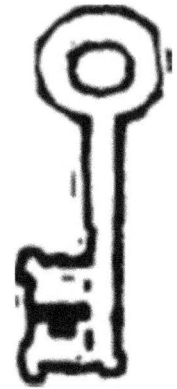

Topics for Further Study

- Do research to learn about Americans who lived in Europe in the last quarter of the nineteenth century. Why were they there? What were their lives like? How accurately did James portray these people and the times in which they lived?

- Discuss your opinion of Isabel's decision to return to Gilbert. What do you think were her motivations for doing this? Do you think the decision was a wise one, or not? Why or why not?

- Discuss James's ideas about Americans as depicted in the novel. According to James, what traits are distinctly American? To what extent do Americans today reflect these traits? What other traits would you consider to be characteristic of today's Americans?

- Ralph thought that a large inheritance would enable Isabel to fulfill her potential and have a good life. Many people today feel the same way—that having money is the key to happiness and fulfillment. What role did Isabel's inheritance play in her life? Would she have been better off without the money? What lessons can readers draw from her experience?

- Write an epilogue for the book, telling what the rest of Isabel's life is like. What happens to her independent spirit? How do her relationships with her husband and stepdaughter evolve? How much happiness does Isabel find?

Social and Emotional Maturation

Isabel's social and emotional development is thrown into high relief by James's contrast of American and European natures. Yet Isabel's experiences and the wisdom she gains from them are certainly not unique to American women coming of age in European society. Isabel's naiveté is common among young women in all cultures, which is one reason why the novel remains popular. It is almost a rule that young women make poor romantic choices. In fact, they often make exactly the mistake that Isabel makes: they choose a man who is charming and seductive, yet self-centered, over one who is less worldly but more substantial and caring. This oft-repeated error of youth has been the subject of many works of literature. Perhaps the best-known is Jane Austen's *Sense and Sensibility*, which contrasts the naive Marianne and her wiser sister, Elinor.

In *The Portrait of a Lady*, James uses one theme, the contrasts between Americans and Europeans, to intensify another, more universal theme of a woman's development from naive youth to mature wisdom as she suffers the consequences of a poor romantic choice.

Style

Psychological Realism

James is considered the foremost author of psychological realism, a subcategory of American realism.

The Realist period in American literature followed Romanticism, a movement that produced stories of idealized love and that elevated emotion above reason. The harsh realities of the Civil War suddenly made Romanticism irrelevant. The year of the war's end, 1865, marks the end of the Romantic period and the beginning of American realism.

Realism got its name from the fact that its stories depicted realistic characters in believable, lifelike situations. Heroes and heroines were not larger than life; they were often "just plain folks" that readers could identify with. And these characters faced problems similar to those that real people faced—neither melodramatic and overblown nor magically solved by some unexpected and incredible twist of the plot. These stories were told in straightforward, objective prose that sought to engage readers' minds more than their emotions.

James was one of the leading authors of American realism, along with Mark Twain (who is sometimes classified as a regionalist) and William Dean Howells. Some critics complained that there was nothing realistic about James's stories, in which everyone was wealthy and refined. The simple answer is that James never pretended to write about all elements of human society. He wrote about the wealthy because it was the wealthy and their problems that he was familiar with and interested in.

In addition to limiting his subject matter to the lives of the wealthy, James also built his stories on the psychology of his characters. The stories are about what goes on inside characters' minds, how they experience and think about the things that happen to them, and how these inner experiences change them as people. The events that happen in James's stories are included not primarily for their own importance but because they shed light on the minds and personalities of the characters. *The Portrait of a Lady* is the story of Isabel's mind and how it shapes her destiny and her character. For this and other masterful tales of human psychology, James is considered the father of psychological realism.

Point of View

Modern readers are unlikely to take special notice of point of view in *The Portrait of a Lady*, but James's contemporaries did. While the point of view that James uses is common today, it was an innovation in James's time. In fact, it was an innovation to which James was an important contributor.

In most novels published before this one, the

author was a prominent narrator—almost a character. In addition to telling the story, the author-narrator often inserted asides directly addressing the reader, commenting on the characters' actions, and so on. This gives fiction an artificial quality; the reader never forgets that he or she is being told a story that has been invented and shaped by the author. To put it another way, the author is always "visible" as an intermediary between the characters and the reader.

This technique of storytelling was not suitable to realism, which strove to make the story seem lifelike rather than artificial. James wanted readers to observe his characters directly and to interpret characters' actions themselves, just as they would observe people around them in life. This meant that he had to get himself as author out of the picture. So, while *The Portrait of a Lady* does have a third-person narrator, that narrator is not James and does not intrude into the story. Instead of readers learning about Isabel through a narrator's comments and interpretations, readers learn about Isabel directly by observing Isabel's actions.

James was influenced by George Eliot, who was a pioneer in minimizing the author's role in the story, but he developed the new point of view into the form that is common today.

Historical Context

Although the period known as the Enlightenment took place a century before *The Portrait of a Lady* was written, the Enlightenment is the historical period that most influences the novel's characters and its story. Isabel, especially, is a product of Enlightenment ideas.

The Enlightenment was a philosophical, political, and literary movement that swept Europe and the United States throughout the 1700s. Its major feature was the elevation of reason and scientific observation above the mysticism and superstition of the Middle Ages. All traditions and conventions, from the religious to the political and social, were reevaluated. No idea or authority was to be accepted blindly or merely because it had been accepted in the past; only those ideas that could be supported by reason or proven scientifically were considered valid.

The idea of the superiority of the intellect led to the idea that human beings were essentially good and were capable of improving and even perfecting themselves. People did not need religious dogma or political authorities to tell them how to live; they had the ability, and therefore the right, to make their own decisions. It is easy to see how such thinking led directly to an emphasis on the political and social rights of individuals.

Compare & Contrast

- **Late 1800s:** England, France, and Italy are the cultural epicenters of the Western world. England produces the best literature and drama; Italy leads in art and architecture; and French style and society are considered the height of sophistication. The United States is viewed as a sort of cultural country cousin to Europe; its arts and culture are considered far inferior to those of the Continent.
  Today: The United States is the cultural pace-setter for the world. American movies, television, music, fashions, and lifestyles are in demand and emulated, not only in Europe but around the globe.

- **Late 1800s:** Most wealthy Americans made their money in industry during the Industrial Revolution of the early 1800s. Factory owners and railroad developers are among those who have amassed huge fortunes. Many of the wealth-producing ventures are family-owned and passed down from father to son. The gap between the rich and poor is growing, as the rich get richer and the poor struggle to maintain a decent lifestyle in an economy producing more and more expensive goods.

Today: Many of the new wealthiest Americans made their money in the high-tech boom of the late 1990s and in other businesses, such as finance, that benefited from it. Most wealth-producing companies are publicly owned, and scandal erupts in 2001 when many of these companies suddenly fail, costing stockholders billions, while top executives continue to receive multi-million-dollar salaries.

- **Late 1800s:** Women do not have the right to vote in the United States or in England. In England, voting rights have long been limited to wealthy men, but they are gradually being extended to more men.

    Today: In both the United States and Great Britain, all men and women have the right to vote.

In *The Portrait of a Lady*, Isabel and the other American characters are products of the Enlightenment whose lives show how completely these ideas were adopted in the United States and how strong their influence still was a century later. It was the big ideas of the Enlightenment that fueled the American Revolution and forever shaped what it meant to be an American. Hence, Isabel takes for granted that she should be able to make her own decisions in life and to do what she feels is best, regardless of social conventions or other people's opinions.

Enlightenment ideas actually first took shape in Europe, but they never fully took hold in England, which is home to most of the novel's European characters. The French Revolution followed the American war of independence and represented the victory of Enlightenment ideas in France. But the English monarchy, Parliament, and ruling class defended themselves against the rising tide of democracy and individualism around them. England never had a revolution. Old ideas about authority and tradition were never swept cleanly away. In the late 1800s, when *The Portrait of a Lady* was written and takes place, England was still very much a society based on wealth, class, tradition, and the supremacy of society over the individual; and it was still consolidating its rule over a vast empire of subject peoples. In stark contrast to America, England saw democracy as a radical ideology and a threat.

Characters such as Ralph and Lord Warburton find Isabel's independence and individualism captivating because Isabel is a captivating young woman who clearly is not a threat. These men, although they reflect European ideas in their own lives, find Isabel's ways refreshing—as long as they are expressed by a lovely young woman and not by an angry mob. To the darker personalities of

Madame Merle and Gilbert Osmond, on the other hand, Isabel's new and different ideas make her an adversary. She is not one of them—she does not value the same things or follow the same conventions—and therefore their impulse is to set themselves against her in some way, just as their government and their society has long set itself against the ideas she represents.

Critical Overview

When *The Portrait of a Lady* was published, James was a well-known and respected author whose story *Daisy Miller* was enjoying great popularity. *The Portrait of a Lady* was widely reviewed, and most reviews, including those in the leading American publications, were positive.

Horace E. Scudder reviewed *The Portrait of a Lady* for *Atlantic*, in which the novel was serialized before its book publication. Scudder's review focuses almost exclusively on what he calls the story's "consistency," by which he means that the novel's "characters, the situations, the incidents, are all true to the law of their own being." Scudder's single complaint is that he does not like the novel's ending. Simply put, he objects to James's sending Isabel back to Gilbert. Isabel deserves better than this, Scudder insists, and when one reads of her return to the dastardly Gilbert, "one's indignation is moved."

An anonymous review for *Harper's*, the other leading American literary magazine of the day, calls *The Portrait of a Lady* a "long and fragmentary but profoundly interesting tale."

In the *Nation*, W. C. Brownell calls the novel "an important work, the most important Mr. James has thus far written" and "his masterpiece." Brownell, too, has one complaint, though he voices it hesitantly: he thinks the story lacks excitement.

He writes:

> *The Portrait of a Lady* … is not only outside of the category of the old romance of which *Tom Jones*, for example, may stand as the type, but also dispenses with the dramatic movement and passionate interest upon which the later novelists, from Thackeray to Thomas Hardy, have relied. In a sense, and to a certain extent, Turgeneff [Turgenev] may be said to be Mr. James's master, but even a sketch or a study by Turgeneff is turbulence itself beside the elaborate placidity of these 519 pages.

Brownell then calls his complaint "ungracious" and "hypercritical," and concludes that *The Portrait of a Lady* is the best piece of realistic fiction published to date.

A long, unhappy review in the British magazine *Blackwood's*, by Margaret Oliphant, is fascinating for its litany of political and cultural objections and its paucity of comment on the book's literary merit or lack thereof. Two brief excerpts from Oliphant's review sum up her attitude. Of James, she writes:

> This gentleman's work in the world seems to be a peculiar one. It is to record and set fully before us the predominance of the great American

> race, and the manner in which it has overrun and conquered the Old World.

This is an interesting view of an American who chose to live his life in Europe. But Oliphant is certain in it, and describes Isabel Archer as

> the young lady who suddenly appears in the doorway of an old English country-house, inhabited like most other desirable places by American tenants ... fresh from her native country, prepared to take instant possession of her birthright as explorer, discoverer, and conqueror of the old country,—and, in fact, reducing the gentlemen who meet her into instant subjection in the course of half an hour.

The Portrait of a Lady has grown in stature in the century and a quarter since its publication. It continues to be included among James's best novels, among the greatest novels written in English, and even among the greatest works in all of world literature. George Perkins writes in his *Reference Guide to American Literature* article on James, "In *The Portrait of a Lady*, *The Wings of the Dove*, *The Ambassadors*, and *The Golden Bowl*, the theme of partial perspectives (which involves often the theme of too late awareness) merges with the international theme to provide the substance of James's most lasting achievement."

The chapter on *The Portrait of a Lady* in the Twayne's United States Authors Series volume *Henry James: The Early Novels* pays high tribute to the novel while acknowledging its impact on literature to come:

> *The Portrait of a Lady* shows James in the fullness of his powers. The sheer beauty, grace, and assurance of the writing, almost startling in the opening description of Gardencourt, and sustained for five-hundred pages, reveal James at a new level of achievement as a prose stylist; and the richness of his character portraits and intensity of his engagement with his subject are of a kind that belong to history-making novels. *The Portrait of a Lady* is history-making literally. The opening account of Gardencourt, in which a densely solid actuality has begun to dissolve into psychological atmosphere, shows literary impressionism at a high stage of development. And Isabel's chapter-length meditative vigil, projected in a long, dramatic interior monologue, lays the foundations of the stream-of-consciousness novel of Joyce, Dorothy Richardson, and Virginia Woolf.

What Do I Read Next?

- James's *The Ambassadors* (1903) provides a counterpoint to *The Portrait of a Lady*. *The Ambassadors* is considered one of the finest works from the later period of his career and James himself considered it his masterpiece. Like the earlier work, *The Ambassadors* is a psychological novel that portrays Americans in Europe, but the later work clearly shows a shift in James's attitudes toward Americans.

- James was well known as a travel writer. In 1993, the Library of America published a two-volume collection of his travel essays: *Henry James: Collected Travel Writings;*

Great Britain and America and *Henry James: Collected Travel Writings; The Continent*.

- American author Edith Wharton was a friend of Henry James, and the work of the two is often compared. Wharton's *The Age of Innocence* (1920) is often recommended as a paired reading with *The Portrait of a Lady* because the novels deal with similar subject matter and are written in a similar style, yet Wharton's is written from a distinctly female point of view.

- Isabel in *The Portrait of a Lady* can be compared with Bathsheba Everdene, the heroine of *Far from the Madding Crowd*, written by Thomas Hardy and first published in 1874. Ranked as a Victorian classic, Hardy's story of a woman farmer and her three suitors is similar in subject matter to *The Portrait of a Lady* but is written in an earlier and very different style.

- George Eliot, an early master of psychological realism, was one of James's primary literary influences. Dorothea Brooke, protagonist of Eliot's masterpiece *Middlemarch* (1871), is another character who has often been compared to Isabel

Archer. Like Isabel, Dorothea marries men her family and friends do not approve of.

Sources

Brownell, W. C., Review of *The Portrait of a Lady*, in the *Nation*, Vol. 34, February 2, 1882, pp. 102–03.

Gale, Robert L., "Henry James," in *Dictionary of Literary Biography*, Vol. 12, *American Realists and Naturalists*, Gale Research, 1982, pp. 297–326.

James, Henry, *The Portrait of a Lady*, edited by Robert D. Bamberg, W. W. Norton, 1975.

Oliphant, Margaret, Review of *The Portrait of a Lady*, in *Blackwood's Edinburgh Magazine*, Vol. 131, March 1882, pp. 374–83.

Perkins, George, "James, Henry," in *Reference Guide to American Literature*, 3d ed., edited by Jim Kamp, St. James Press, 1994.

" *The Portrait of a Lady*: The Caging of the Beautiful Striver," in *Henry James: The Early Novels*, Twayne's United States Authors Series, 1999.

Review of *The Portrait of a Lady*, in *Harper's*, Vol. 64, February 1882, p. 474.

Scudder, Horace E., Review of *The Portrait of a Lady*, in the *Atlantic Monthly*, Vol. 49, January 1882, pp. 127–28.

Further Reading

Anesko, Michael, ed., *Letters, Fictions, Lives: Henry James and William Dean Howells*, Oxford University Press, 1997.

> This selection of correspondence between James and Howells, two of the luminaries of American realism, provides insight into how both authors worked.

Bloom, Harold, ed., *Henry James's "The Portrait of a Lady"*, Chelsea House, 1987.

> Respected critic Bloom gathered criticism and essays from an array of James scholars for this volume.

Edel, Leon, "The Myth of America in *The Portrait of a Lady*," in the *Henry James Review*, Vol. 7, 1986, pp. 8–17.

> This scholarly journal is wholly devoted to James and his work, and volume seven contains several articles on *The Portrait of a Lady*. Edel, a James scholar, analyzes James's rendering of the United States in the novel.

James, Henry, *Henry James: Autobiography*, Criterion Books, 1956.

> This edition brings together all three

volumes of James's autobiography: *A Small Boy and Others*, originally published in 1913; *Notes of a Son and Brother*, 1914; and *The Middle Years*, 1917.

Skrupskelis, Ignas K., and Elizabeth M. Berkeley, eds., *William and Henry James: Selected Letters*, University Press of Virginia, 1997.

> The editors have collected some of the private correspondence of the two famous brothers, William, the philosopher, and Henry, the writer.

Milton Keynes UK
Ingram Content Group UK Ltd.
UKHW022012230824
447344UK00012B/727